FABERGE

Fantasies & Treasures

FABERGÉ

Fantasies & Treasures

GÉZA VON HABSBURG

FABERGÉ CO.

IN ASSOCIATION WITH

UNIVERSE PUBLISHING

FRONT COVER:
LILIES OF THE VALLEY EGG

BACK COVER:
BASKET OF LILIES OF THE VALLEY

FRONTISPIECE:
CZAREVITCH EGG

PAGES 6–7:
BRIDAL FAN

Fabergé Fantasies and Treasures is published upon the occasion of the exhibition *Fabergé in America*, organized by the Fine Arts Museums of San Francisco and made possible by FABERGÉ CO.

First published in the United States of America in 1996
by UNIVERSE PUBLISHING
A Division of Rizzoli International Publications, Inc.
300 Park Avenue South
New York, NY   10010

96 97 98 99/10 9 8 7 6 5 4 3 2 1

Library of Congress Catalog Card Number: 95-61883

Design and typography by Nai Chang

PRINTED IN SINGAPORE

CONTENTS

FOREWORD

Fabergé Fantasies and Treasures is published as a companion to the catalog for *Fabergé in America,* a nationwide museum exhibition sponsored with great pride by FABERGÉ CO. This first comprehensive showing of Carl Fabergé's art in this country reflects America's fascination for one of the best-known artist-jewelers of all times.

This book, written by the exhibition's curator and renowned Fabergé expert Dr. Géza von Habsburg, portrays some of the most celebrated works of art crafted by this legendary artist that have been acquired by American collectors over the past 100 years. It focuses in part on the objects that have become synonymous with the Fabergé name, the priceless Easter eggs, the majority of which today are in American hands. In addition, the book features Fabergé's objects of fantasy in gold, enamel, and hardstone, for which he is so justly renowned.

Fabergé's innovative designs and unsurpassed attention to detail are the master's enduring legacy to our times. It is our hope that exhibitions and books such as this one will enhance our appreciation of Fabergé's genius.

PATRICK J. CHOËL

PRESIDENT, CHIEF EXECUTIVE OFFICER

FABERGÉ CO.

FABERGÉ'S
ASCENT TO
FAME

The exhibition . . . features so many riches, so many marvelous,

extraordinarily artistic objects that one would not know where to fix one's glance. . . .

It is difficult to imagine anything more spectacular and

at the same time exquisite.[1]

These laudatory sentences were written about an exhibition of Fabergé's creations for the Russian Imperial family held in 1902. In just over thirty years this Russian master had risen from obscurity to the position of leading court jeweler and gold- and silversmith (fig. 1).

Carl Fabergé was born in St. Petersburg in 1846, son of a little known, but respectable, jeweler of French Protestant extraction. His early education took place in Russia. In 1860 his father moved to Dresden, Germany, leaving his affairs in the hands of trusted friends. Over a period of four years, Fabergé was instructed in the art of running a business. During an educational trip to Western Europe he absorbed all the newest trends and styles in goldsmithing, returning to Russia in 1864, brimming with novel ideas, and joining the staff of his father's jewelry shop in St. Petersburg. His name first appears on the city rosters in 1866 as having obtained a temporary license allowing him to do business. This was ratified a year later.

1. Quoted from Marina Lopato, "New Insights into Fabergé from Russian Documents," in Géza von Habsburg and Marina Lopato, *Fabergé: Imperial Jeweler,* Harry N. Abrams Inc., New York, 1994, p. 69.

FIGURE 1. CARL FABERGÉ SORTING PRECIOUS STONES
PHOTOGRAPH BY HUGO OEBERG, ST. PETERSBURG, C. 1900. PHOTOGRAPH COURTESY OF THE AUTHOR

Nothing has survived of Fabergé's beginnings. We may assume that from 1872, when Carl Fabergé married and took over his father's shop, until 1882, he produced traditional jewelry in the then fashionable Russian style. At the same time he studied the time-honored techniques of the great jewelers and goldsmiths of the past. The school which provided Fabergé and his craftsmen with unrivaled sources of inspiration was the Jewelry Gallery of the Hermitage in St. Petersburg, the greatest treasury of Western art in Russia. The Romanov crown jewels and the prized collections of precious objects the Russian czars amassed over the centuries were stored here under the care of the Imperial Cabinet. With time Fabergé made himself indispensable to this body, voluntarily repairing deficient objects, appraising new acquisitions, and helping to organize the collection. Beginning in 1866, he sold modest pieces of jewelry to the Cabinet, competing with the established court jewelers of the time. He also undertook the time-consuming labor of restoring the vast hoard of fourth-century B.C. gold jewels and objects which had been found in the tombs of Scythian chieftains in the Crimea, then deposited in the Hermitage of the Winter Palace. This was to bear rich fruit.

Following the example of his peers in London and Paris, who had introduced the fashion of archaeological revival in jewelry, Fabergé asked permission to copy a number of these Greek gold antiquities. His re-creations were first shown in 1882 at the great Pan-Slavic exhibition held in Moscow under the patronage of Czar Alexander III. His work caught the eye of the Czarina Maria Feodorovna, who acquired a pair of cicada-shaped cufflinks. Fabergé was awarded a gold medal for his exhibits, with, as sign of Imperial favor, the right to wear it on the ribbon of the Order of St. Stanislas. The press wrote enthusiastically about this new craftsman, whose jewels captured the imagination of the public with their exquisite workmanship:

> *Among the jewellery makers there is a man who made it a point to bring the business back to its lofty stand. . . . As we see, Mr. Fabergé opens up a new era in the art of jewellery. We wish him all the best in his efforts to bring back into the realm of art what once used to be part of it. We hope that from now on, thanks to our renowned jeweller, the value of the objects will be measured not only by the value of the precious stones, not by wealth alone, but by their artistic form as well.*[2]

During the years that followed, Carl Fabergé and his younger brother Agathon designed diadems, brooches, flower sprays, and stomachers in the prevalent French eighteenth-century style. However, at the same time both shied away from these traditional adornments of the 1870s and 1880s, which were over-laden with diamonds. Inspired by his success in 1882, Fabergé decided to become an artist-jeweler, thus setting out on a new course that was to make his fame. The first examples of this new art appear in 1884 or 1885 in the form of enameled gold snuffboxes inspired by originals of the eighteenth century. They show a craftsmanship that had been lost for many generations due to the upheavals of the French Revolution. The Imperial Cabinet was to order many of these for presentation purposes, often supplying its own diamonds.

Simultaneously, Fabergé created the first Easter egg of a series that was to become his chief legacy to the world of the objects of fantasy. Favorably impressed with these proofs of his jeweler's qualifications, Alexander III award-

2. Ibid. pp. 56–67.

ed Fabergé the title of Supplier by Special Appointment to the Imperial Court in 1885. In this pivotal year Fabergé was honored with two further distinctions: he received his first international recognition in the form of a Gold Medal for an exhibition in Nürnberg, Germany, for the same Greek revivalist jewelry previously shown in Moscow; at the same time the Czar underscored Fabergé's special status with the Imperial family by bestowing on him a permanent order for a yearly Imperial Easter egg.

Fabergé never looked back. Signs of recognition from the Imperial family followed one upon the other: the Order of St. Stanislas 1st Class (1889); a title of Appraiser of the Imperial Cabinet and a commission for a series of snuffboxes and jewels to accompany the Czarevich on his world tour (1890); the Silver Anniversary clock of the Czar and Czarina (1891); the Golden Anniversary presents of the King and Queen of Denmark (1892); the betrothal presents of Nicholas and Alexandra (1894).

The year 1896 marked another milestone in Fabergé's career. For the coronation of Czar Nicholas II a large number of official presents were ordered from the house of Fabergé; he was awarded the State Emblem for his participation in an exhibition at Nizhny Novgorod and obtained the Order of St. Stanislas 2nd Class. In 1897 Fabergé exhibited at the Nordic Exhibition in Stockholm and received the Royal Warrant from the courts of Sweden and Norway.

The turn of the century brought about Fabergé's greatest triumph. By Imperial command he participated in the 1900 Exposition Universelle in Paris, was awarded a Gold Medal, the Cross of the Legion of Honor, and more important, obtained international fame.

FIGURE 2. FABERGÉ HOUSE AT 24 BOLSHAYA MORSKAYA STREET, ST. PETERSBURG, C. 1910
PHOTOGRAPH COURTESY OF THE AUTHOR

A lavish building in St. Petersburg (fig. 2) remains a symbol of the firm's
renown. Fabergé's workshops (fig. 3) produced an apparently never-ending
stream of objects of virtuoso craftsmanship, most of them sold in the firm's

FIGURE 3. THE FABERGÉ ENAMELING WORKSHOP, ST. PETERSBURG, C. 1905
PHOTOGRAPH COURTESY FERSMAN MINERALOGICAL INSTITUTE, MOSCOW

FIGURE 4. FABERGÉ SHOWROOMS, ST. PETERSBURG, C. 1905
PHOTOGRAPH COURTESY OF THE AUTHOR

local showrooms (fig. 4). Czars and grand dukes, most of Europe's royalty and aristocracy, even some of the New World's robber barons became faithful clients of the Russian craftsman.

IMPERIAL
EASTER EGGS

PLATE I. SPRING FLOWERS EGG

Since the beginning of the second millennium, the egg in its various forms has symbolized Easter and the Resurrection of Christ for the Orthodox Russian. From peasant to Emperor, from the simplest painted shell to the most lavish extravaganza in the form of a jeweled object, eggs have for centuries been presented or exchanged with the traditional three Easter kisses and the ritual "Christ is Risen," "Yes Christ is truly risen." A number of eighteenth-century Easter eggs preserved in the treasury of the Hermitage attest to this tradition within the Imperial family.

Legend surrounds the creation of Fabergé's first Imperial Easter egg. Its inception is traditionally attributed to Czar Alexander III. Following a request of the Czar, Fabergé is thought to have used an eighteenth-century egg in the treasury of the Kings of Denmark as a prototype, in a desire to please the Danish-born Empress. Recent discoveries would on the contrary indicate that the first egg was an initiative of Fabergé's dating back to 1884, possibly based on an original he may have seen in the Dresden Green Vaults.[3] This so-called "first egg" (The Forbes Magazine Collection, New York), shaped as a hen within an enameled white shell, is not listed among the invoices and orders of the Imperial Cabinet. These recently discovered files mention five hitherto unknown eggs by Fabergé,

---

3. For the date of the first egg, see Marina Lopato, "A Few Remarks Regarding Imperial Easter Eggs," op.cit., pp. 71ff. For the prototype of the first egg from the Dresden Green Vaults, see auction Habsburg, Feldman, Geneva, November 16, 1988, lot 255.

thus upsetting the generally accepted chronology.[4] Among these, an egg described as "In 1888—Angel pulling a chariot with an egg—1500 rubles" probably survives, unrecognized, in an American collection, since it may have been among the objects sold by Armand Hammer in 1934 at Lord & Taylor ("No. 4524—Miniature Amour [ed. Cupid] holding wheelbarrow with Easter egg. Made by Fabergé"). The others may possibly have had a similar fate.

The earliest Fabergé eggs are mostly derivative. Among the eggs in American collections, the shell of the *Spring Flowers Egg* (pl. 1) is a pastiche of an eighteenth-century bonbonnière, the *Renaissance Egg* (pl. 2) is modeled after a late seventeenth-century casket in the Dresden Green Vaults, and the *Orange Tree Egg* (pl. 3) is inspired by a French nineteenth-century clockwork orange tree with singing birds. Yet in spite of these similitudes, upon closer inspection all of Fabergé's creations are original and none are slavish copies. Certainly the fact that they contain some form of surprise sets even these earliest eggs apart from their prototypes.

It is interesting to note that Fabergé was strongly dependent on the whims of the Imperial Cabinet when designing the egg of 1885. Extensive consultations about questions of detail were necessary before Fabergé received approval for his project. Later, Fabergé was to complain about the bureaucracy of the Imperial Cabinet whose members "knew nothing about art," yet their commissions "were always very urgent." Mercifully, Fabergé's Imperial Easter eggs were soon out of their sphere of influence, for the Czar granted him total liberty as to

---

4. "In 1885—Easter egg of white enamel, the crown is set with rubies, diamonds and rose diamonds—4151 rubles (including 2 ruby eggs—2700 rubles); in 1886—the hen taking a sapphire out of the wicker basket - 2968 rubles (including the sapphire—1800 rubles); in 1887—Easter egg with a clock decorated with brilliants, sapphires and rose diamonds—2160 rubles; in 1889 —pearl egg—981 rubles."

PLATE 2. RENAISSANCE EGG

PLATE 3.
ORANGE TREE EGG

their creation. The only precepts were that they should be egg-shaped, contain a surprise, and not be repetitive in theme.

The Imperial Easter eggs were very much conversation pieces at a time of slow communications. Both the public and the Imperial family might speculate as to the nature of the next egg, yet no questioning could prize the secret from Fabergé. *"Your Majesty will be satisfied"* would be his laconic answer. To a persistent lady who insisted on learning about the form of the forthcoming egg, Fabergé is said to have replied: *"Next year the eggs will be square!"*

Fabergé is believed to have created eleven eggs as Easter presents from Czar Alexander III to his wife Maria Feodorovna between 1884 and his death in 1894. A further forty-four eggs, two for each year, were apparently made between 1895 and 1916 for Czar Nicholas II, who, as a dutiful son, continued the tradition of giving his mother an egg, adding one for his wife, Alexandra Feodorovna. One of the eggs of 1917, never presented since the Czar was by that time a prisoner, was discovered by an American dealer in the Shanghai flea market.[5] Of a total of fifty-six eggs, forty-four survive and two are known only from photographs.

As Fabergé's fame asserted itself, the design of the Imperial eggs became more and more ambitious and required longer planning. Some of them are known to have taken up to two years of preparation. The subjects of the eggs were mostly connected with the family and with events in the Imperial household in order to "give some meaning to the gift, but political events were, of course, avoided." Thus, for example, the celebrated *Coronation Egg* (pl. 4) of 1897 contains a

---

5. The *Night Egg,* or *Twilight Egg,* was sold at Christie's in Geneva, November 10, 1976, lot 184.

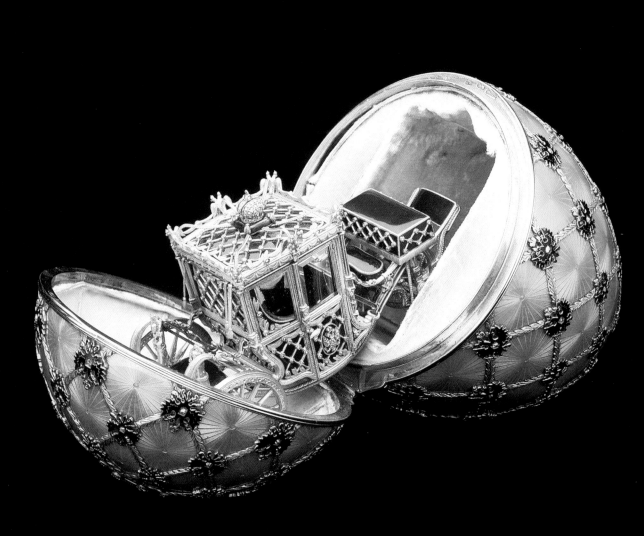

OPPOSITE:
PLATE 4.
CORONATION EGG

RIGHT:
PLATE 5.
PETER THE GREAT EGG

PLATE 6. NAPOLEONIC EGG

miniature replica of the coach, which took fifteen months to perfect, in which
Czarina Alexandra Feodorovna rode into Moscow preceding the 1896 coronation; the *Peter the Great Egg* (pl. 5) of 1903, modeled after the statue of Czar Peter
by Falconet, commemorates the festivities marking the two-hundredth anniversary of the founding of the city of St. Petersburg; and the *Napoleonic Egg* (pl. 6)
of 1912 celebrates the one-hundredth anniversary of the victory of the Russian
armies over Napoleon.

PLATE 7. CAUCASUS EGG

The Easter eggs destined for Czarina Maria Feodorovna usually contained surprises connected with her life. Thus the *Caucasus Egg* (pl. 7) of 1893 is painted with miniatures of a mountain lodge where her younger son was convalescing; the *Danish Palaces Egg* (pl. 8) of 1895 contains a screen painted with her palaces and yachts; and the *Gatchina Palace Egg* of 1902 (The Walters Art Gallery, Baltimore) opens to reveal a miniature replica of her summer palace.

PLATE 8. DANISH PALACES EGG
(DETAIL ABOVE)

PLATE 9. HEART SURPRISE FRAME

The Easter presents for Czarina Alexandra Feodorovna usually involved images of her beloved children and of her husband. The surprise for the lost 1897 egg is a heart-shaped frame (pl. 9) opening as a three-leaf clover and painted with miniatures of Grand Duchess Olga, together with her proud parents; from the *Lilies of the Valley Egg* (pl. 10) of 1898 emerge the miniatures of the Czarina's two eldest daughters, Olga and Tatiana, together with their father Nicholas II; the *Pansy Egg* (pl. 11) of 1899 contains a heart-shaped frame with eleven concealed miniatures of the Imperial children together with their parents, uncles, and aunts; finally, on a more somber note, the two eggs for 1915 are both "Red Cross Eggs" (pl. 12) underlining the role that the Czarina and her two eldest daughters played as Sisters of Mercy, tending the wounded in a hospital at Czarskoie Selo.

The Easter eggs were the pride of Fabergé's firm, and also their main concern. With only one exception—an egg crafted in the main jewelry workshop of August Holmström—all eggs were the direct responsibility of Fabergé and of his head workmaster. From 1884 until 1903 the head workmaster was Mikhail Perkhin; from 1903 until 1916 the position was held by Henrik Wigström. Their inventions are a matter for conjecture. Certainly the early eggs were probably conceived by the Fabergé brothers. After 1893, when Franz Bierbäum joined the firm as chief designer, apparently most of the ideas were his (*"About fifty or sixty of these eggs were made and I composed more than half of them myself."*). The eggs were displayed to the public at the St. Petersburg shop during the days preceding their presentation. On Good Friday, Carl Fabergé would travel to Czarskoie Selo, while the craftsmen would remain at their places until he returned, in case "anything unexpected happened." Later, Fabergé's eldest son Eugène would assist in

LEFT:
PLATE 10. LILIES OF THE VALLEY
EGG

OPPOSITE:
PLATE 11. PANSY EGG

PLATE 12.
RED CROSS EGG
(DETAIL BELOW)

the presentation of one of the two eggs. When the Dowager Empress resided at Livadia, her egg was presumably conveyed to her by train.

There is a touching personal note attached to the presentation of the 1914 *Pink Cameo Egg* (pl. 13) to the Dowager Empress, who described the scene in a letter to her sister, the Queen Mother Alexandra (widow of King Edward VII):

> *He* (Czar Nicholas II) *wrote me a most charming letter and presented me with a most beautiful Easter egg. Fabergé brought it to me himself. It is a true* chef d'oeuvre *in pink enamel and inside a* porte-chaise *carried by two negroes with Empress Catherine in it wearing a little crown on her head. You wind it up and then the negroes walk: it is an unbelievably beautiful and superbly fine piece of work. Fabergé is the greatest genius of our time, I also told him:* Vous êtes un génie incomparable.

A word from Dowager Empress Maria Feodorovna concerning the *Cross of St. George Egg* (The Forbes Magazine Collection, New York) presented in 1916, while Nicholas II was at the Stavka with the troops, has also survived. She wrote: *"Christ has indeed arisen! I kiss you three times and thank you with all my heart for your dear cards and lovely egg with miniatures, which dear old Fabergé brought himself. It is beautiful. . . . Your fondly loving old Mama."*

Fabergé's Imperial Easter eggs were publicly exhibited in Russia only once, in 1902, along with other Fabergé objects belonging to members of the Imperial family at the von Dervis mansion in St. Petersburg. The press was lavish with its praise. In 1916 a laudatory article was written about them in the fashionable magazine *Stoliza i Usadba*. For the Imperial family, while Fabergé was their leading jeweler, his objects were considered as part of their furnishings, and there-

PLATE 13. PINK CAMEO EGG

fore not highlighted in any special way. Judging from contemporary photographs of the Mauve Salon at the Alexander Palace, Alexandra Feodorovna exhibited her eggs in a corner cabinet flanked by Art Nouveau glass. The Dowager Empress's Easter eggs were kept at her Anichkov Palace.

Lavish Easter eggs by Fabergé were, of course, not only the prerogative of the Imperial family. A wealthy gold mining magnate, Alexander F. Kelch, commissioned seven eggs for his wife Barbara between 1898 and 1903, similar to those made for the Czar. The earliest among these was another "hen egg" (pl. 14), a variant on the theme of the Imperial 1884 egg, both in The Forbes Magazine Collection, of which one further version in lapis lazuli exists in the India Early Minshall Collection at the Cleveland Museum of Art (pl. 15). The only egg ordered by a non-Russian was made for American-born Consuelo Vanderbilt, Duchess of Marlborough, in 1902, a pink enamel egg shaped as a Louis XVI clock (pl. 16).

Fabergé's creativity was without limits when it came to designing egg shaped objects as alternative Easter presents. An ingenious egg containing a perfume flacon (pl. 17) is similar to an item which appears on an inventory of objects confiscated from the Dowager Empress in 1917. An ovoid frame (pl. 18) with a miniature portrait of the same Empress descends from her daughter, Grand Duchess Xenia, and has also found a home in an American private collection. The genius of Fabergé is perhaps most palpable in the multitude of miniature Easter eggs (pl. 19) created over the five decades of the firm's existence. Several thousand of these were crafted in the various jewelry workshops, and yet there are virtually no repetitions.

PLATE 14. KELCH HEN EGG

PLATE 15. LAPIS EGG

OPPOSITE LEFT:
PLATE 16. DUCHESS OF
MARLBOROUGH EGG

OPPOSITE RIGHT:
PLATE 17. PERFUME BOTTLE EGG

RIGHT:
PLATE 18. EGG-SHAPED FRAME
(ENLARGED)

PLATE 19. GROUP OF SIXTEEN MINIATURE EGGS

FABERGÉ
JEWELER

$\mathcal{T}$he Easter eggs represent but a minute fraction of Fabergé's production. More than 150,000 items of jewelry, silver, and of fantasy were designed and executed by the five hundred craftsmen active in St. Petersburg and Moscow. The great majority of jewels were destroyed following the Revolution, and only smaller objects have survived. A group of snowflake brooches (pl. 20 & 21) drawn after nature illustrate Fabergé's preference for innovative designs over expensive materials. These were acquired by financier J. P. Morgan, Jr. in 1905 as presents for his daughters. An elegant pink enameled diamond-set lapel watch (pl. 22) and two pairs of enamel cufflinks (pl. 23 & 24) also escaped destruction due to their low intrinsic value.

PLATES 20. & 21. SNOWFLAKE BROOCHES (ENLARGED)

PLATE 22. PINK ENAMEL LAPEL WATCH

PLATE 23. WHITE ENAMEL CUFFLINKS
PLATE 24. RED ENAMEL CUFFLINKS

FABERGÉ
SILVERSMITH

PLATE 25. SILVER PIKE BOWL

$\mathcal{F}$abergé silver was produced in large quantities both in the Moscow workshops and in a factory situated on the Ekatarinski Canal in St. Petersburg. A substantial percentage of the firm's monumental pieces, including court and presentation silver, was melted down in order to mint silver ingots and rubles in the 1920s. What remains are primarily objects of function which found their way to the West. They include flatware, tea sets, samovars, candlesticks, and a number of realistically rendered animals functioning as table lighters and wine pitchers. A bowl modeled in the shape of a pike (pl. 25) and a decanter formed as a dachshund (pl. 26) show the care with which studies after nature were executed in the silver workshops.

PLATE 26. SILVER DACHSHUND DECANTER

THE
OBJECTS OF
FANTASY

PLATE 27. JADE PRESENTATION BOX

Hardstones

$\mathcal{A}$lthough Fabergé's main sources of profit may have been jewelry and silver, his fame rested essentially on his objects of fantasy, many of which were made of hardstones, often mounted in gold or silver gilt. Fabergé's flowers, hardstone sculptures of animals, folkloristic figures, and objects of relatively small intrinsic value—but of exquisite execution—belong to this body of work.

As of the eighteenth century, Russia's enormous mineral wealth engendered a well-established hardstone-cutting industry with stone cutting centers in Ekatarinenburg, Peterhof, and St. Petersburg. Yet no predecessor, nor contemporary, was able to carve stone with such apparent ease as Fabergé. His craftsmen succeeded in cutting nephrite, a dark green Siberian jade, into wafer-thin, transparent panels, which were mounted into ornate presentation cigarette boxes (pl. 27). The same stone was fashioned into an opening lotus blossom set on a jeweled and enameled gold base (fig. 28) possibly as a commission for the King of Siam; or into a circular tray with rococo-style handles (pl. 29); or into an anniversary clock (pl. 30). A gold-mounted flawless smoky topaz vase (pl. 31) was once a present from Grand Duke Admiral of the Fleet Aleksei Aleksandrovich to his mistress Elizabeth Balletta.

PLATE 28.
VASE IN RENAISSANCE-STYLE MOUNT

PLATE 29. CIRCULAR TRAY

PLATE 30. TWENTY-FIFTH ANNIVERSARY CLOCK

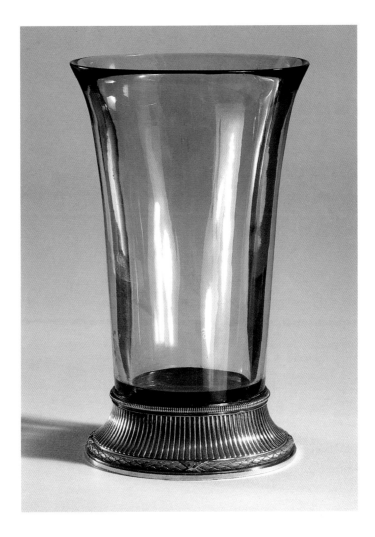

PLATE 31. BALLETTA VASE

Flowers

Fabergé's world of hardstone flowers forms part of a long tradition of bouquets made of precious stones dating back to the eighteenth century, of which several examples exist in the treasury of the Hermitage. His workmasters also acknowledged being influenced by Chinese floral arrangements in semi-precious stones. The firm's most celebrated floral composition, and Empress Alexandra Feodorovna's favorite piece by the master, was *Basket of Lilies of the Valley* (pl. 32) presented to her by the merchants of Nizhny Novgorod in 1896, and which stood on her desk until the Revolution. In this object Fabergé has succeeded in transcending nature, breathing life into inanimate materials, thereby creating an immortal work of art. Perhaps the most daring of flowers, and the most successful, was a *Dandelion* Puff Ball (pl. 33), for which, according to chief designer Bierbaum, Fabergé tied the flower's own fluff onto metal stalks. However, laboratory analysis indicates that his craftsmen also used asbestos fiber to imitate the seeds. Following the taste of the day, some of Fabergé's flowers were designed in the Japanese style, with ikebana or bonsai arrangements growing out of bowenite vases (pl. 34). The largest group of hardstone flowers (pl. 35) in the United States was assembled by India Early Minshall in the 1930s and is on view at the Cleveland Museum of Art. Another ingenious composition is the arrangement of cornflowers standing in an iridescent glass vase (pl. 36).

PLATE 32. BASKET OF LILIES OF THE VALLEY

PLATE 33. DANDELION (PUFF BALL)

PLATE 34. JAPANESE FLORAL COMPOSITION

PLATE 35. GROUP OF FLOWERS IN VASES

PLATE 36. CORNFLOWERS

ANIMALS

Specialists consider Fabergé's miniature animal sculptures to be his foremost
contribution to the arts. The finest of these carvings are lovingly modeled, their
characteristics rendered with much humor. Many of them are closely related to
Japanese netsuke carvings in ivory or wood, of which Fabergé possessed a large
collection. This hardstone fauna numbered many hundreds of examples, from
the domestic to the exotic, mostly carved from Russian minerals mined in the
Caucasus and the Urals. The leading collectors of Fabergé's animals were two
Danish-born sisters; Czarina Maria Feodorovna of Russia, and Queen
Alexandra of Great Britain. A listing of items by Fabergé,
confiscated from the former's Anichkov Palace in 1917, included
over one hundred animal sculptures. The collection of Queen
Elizabeth II, of which Queen Alexandra's zoo forms the nucleus,
counts over two hundred fifty such carvings. Some of the animals of
the Russian Imperial family are now in American hands. These include a
serpentine frog climbing an agate pole (pl. 37), a typical example of
Fabergé's clever handling of hardstones, and a pink marble model of a
draft horse (pl. 38) perfectly rendering the work-horse's heavy shape.
Among other virtuoso carvings is a dancing bear (pl. 39) carved from a
specimen piece of lapis lazuli.

PLATE 37. FROG ON AGATE STAND

PLATE 38. DRAFT HORSE

PLATE 39. DANCING BEAR

FIGURINES

A small group of approximately sixty portrait, character, and folkloristic statuettes also exists, composed of polychrome hardstones. These were favorites of the Imperial family. Mostly in European collections, only a handful have crossed the ocean to the United States. A peasant girl (pl. 40) in a scarlet dress of purpurine was acquired from Fabergé by the English Lord Revelstoke and is now in the Metropolitan Museum of Art; a sailor (pl. 41) whose white outfit is made of agate has become part of the Virginia Museum of Fine Arts' Lillian T. Pratt Collection in Richmond, Virginia.

PLATE 40.
RUSSIAN PEASANT GIRL

PLATE 41. SAILOR

ENAMELS

The most jealously guarded technical secret of the Fabergé workshops, and their main claim to fame, was their transparent, or so-called *guilloché*, enamel. Learned from eighteenth-century snuffboxes and objects in the Imperial treasury, Fabergé and his workmasters perfected this art, and brought it to new summits.

PLATE 42.
GRAY ENAMELED
PRESENTATION
CIGARETTE CASE

PLATE 43.
RED ENAMELED
PRESENTATION
CIGARETTE CASE

Up to seven layers of a glasslike fluid tinted with mineral colors were applied to a metal surface, previously engraved by machine or hand, at decreasing temperatures. Over the years, with much experimentation, Fabergé developed an unparalleled palette of one hundred forty-five hues, from which clients could select. These included an elegant steel gray (pl. 42) and a luscious strawberry red (pl. 43). A coat of transparent orange under the last layer gave white, pink, and pale blue enamels a scintillating oyster-shell effect (pl. 44). To alleviate the

PLATE 44. DIAMOND-SHAPED CLOCK

boredom of large enameled surfaces, Fabergé often applied intricate decorations to his objects, as in his yellow enamel *Coronation Box* (pl. 45). Audacious designs abound, some of them distinctly modern in style (pl. 46). A white enamel cigarette case inset with color discs is surely one of Fabergé's most original inventions (pl. 47).

The most sumptuous pieces were often hand-painted under the last coat of enamel. The upholstery on a miniature Louis XVI-style chair (pl. 48) replicates the effects of Lyons silk fabrics; the opalescent pink enamel panels on a miniature sedan chair (pl. 49) are painted with trophies and flower garlands in sepia; a sumptuous miniature Louis XVI-style frame from the Imperial collections (pl. 50), shaped as a fire screen, contrasts an outer border of opaque white with panels of translucent opalescent white; the pink enamel points of a star-shaped clock (pl. 52) from the Imperial yacht *Polar Star* are decorated with dendritic motifs. Doubtless, one of the most accomplished of enameled objects is a Louis XVI-style box (pl. 51) with panels of pale pink opalescent enamel, each painted with a view of one of the palaces of the Yusupov family. This was a present in 1907 for the twenty-fifth wedding anniversary of Prince and Princess Yusupov from their sons Nicholas and Felix. The latter was to be one of the assassins of Rasputin ten years later.

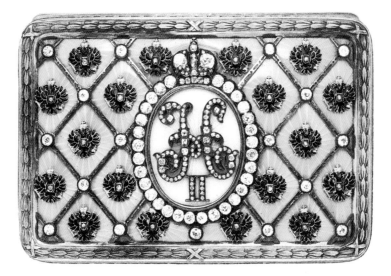

PLATE 45. CORONATION BOX

PLATE 46. *Style-moderne* CLOCK

PLATE 47. AESTHETIC-MOVEMENT CIGARETTE CASE

PLATE 48. MINIATURE CHAIR   PLATE 49. MINIATURE SEDAN CHAIR

PLATE 51. MUSIC BOX

PLATE 50. FIRE-SCREEN FRAME

PLATE 52. POLAR STAR CLOCK

Epilogue

◆ ◆ ◆

*T*he Fabergé workshops were active well into the beginning of World War I. Initially fortune smiled on the Russian armies. Soon however, following disastrous events on the front, it became necessary for the Imperial family, the Court, and Fabergé to share in the war effort. Orders from the Imperial Cabinet and the Court dwindled to a mere trickle. It became fashionable to own objects in base metals. Fabergé made cigarette cases in gunmetal, mugs in brass, cooking pots in copper. His silver factory produced shell casings and grenades. Not even the Czar could save Fabergé's finest craftsmen from being drafted. Following the disastrous outcome of the war, Nicholas II's abdication in 1917 and his murder in 1918, Fabergé closed his shop and fled Russia. He died in Switzerland in 1920, barely surviving the disappearance of the *Belle Époque* and the world of emperors, grand dukes, *demimondaines*, actresses, and ballerinas.

◆ ◆ ◆

Chronology

$\blacklozenge \blacklozenge \blacklozenge$

Select Reading List of Recent Publications in English

◆ ◆ ◆

Booth, John. *The Art of Fabergé*. Secaucus, New Jersey, 1990

Forbes, Christopher, et al. *Fabergé, The Imperial Easter Eggs*. Exhibition Catalogue: San Diego/Moscow, 1989/90

von Habsburg, Géza and Alexander von Solodkoff. *Fabergé: Court Jeweler to the Czars*. Rizzoli, New York, 1979

von Habsburg, Géza *Fabergé*. Vendôme Press, New York, 1987. Exhibition Catalogue: Munich Hypokulturstiftung, 1986/7

von Habsburg, Géza and Marina Lopato. *Fabergé: Imperial Jeweler*. Harry N. Abrams Inc., New York, 1994. Exhibition Catalogue: St. Petersburg, Paris, London, 1993/4

von Habsburg, Géza. *Fabergé: First Impressions*. Harry N. Abrams Inc., New York, 1994

Hill, Gerard. *Fabergé and the Russian Master Goldsmiths*. Wings Books, New York, 1989

Keefe, John. *Masterpieces of Fabergé. The Matilda Geddings Gray Foundation Collection*. New Orleans Museum of Art, 1993

Krairiksh ed. *Fabergé in the Royal Collection*. Thailand n.d. (1984)

Snowman, A. Kenneth. *Carl Fabergé, Goldsmith to the Imperial Court of Russia*. Debrett, London, 1979

Snowman, A. Kenneth. *Fabergé Lost and Found*. Harry N. Abrams Inc., New York, 1993

von Solodkoff, Alexander, ed. *Masterpieces from the House of Fabergé*. Harry N. Abrams Inc., New York, 1984

von Solodkoff, Alexander. *The Art of Carl Fabergé*. Crown Publishers, New York, 1988

Waterfield, Hermione and Christopher Forbes. *C. Fabergé: Imperial Easter Eggs and Other Fantasies*. New York, 1978

For a full Fabergé bibliography, see McCanless, Christel L. *Fabergé and His Works: An Annotated Bibliography of the First Century of his Art*. Scarecrow Press, Metuchen, New Jersey and London, 1994

List of Plates

• • •

14. Kelch Hen Egg
    Gold, enamel, diamonds, rock crystal,
      rubies, suede
    H: 2¼ inches
    Marks: Initials of workmaster Mikhail
      Perkhin, assay mark of St. Petersburg
      before 1896
    The Forbes Magazine Collection, New York

15. Lapis Lazuli Egg
    Gold, enamel, lapis lazuli, pearls,
      diamonds, rubies
    L: 2⁵/₁₆ inches
    The Cleveland Museum of Art, The
      India Early Minshall Collection, 66.436

16. Duchess of Marlborough Egg
    Gold, enamel, diamonds, pearls
    H: 9¼ inches
    Marks: Stamped Fabergé and engraved
      K. Fabergé, 1902, initials of workmaster
      Mikhail Perkhin, assay mark of
      St. Petersburg 1896-1908
    The Forbes Magazine Collection, New York

17. Perfume Bottle Egg
    Agate, gold, enamel, rubies
    H: 4½ inches
    Marks: Fabergé, assay mark of St.
      Petersburg 1896-1908
    New Orleans Museum of Art,
      The Matilda Geddings Gray Foundation
      Collection

18. Imperial Egg-shaped Frame
    Bowenite, enamel, gold, diamonds, ivory
    H: 2¾ inches
    Marks: Fabergé, initials of workmaster
      Mikhail Perkhin, assay mark of
      St. Petersburg before 1896
    Private Collection, California

19. Group of Sixteen Miniature Easter Eggs
    Gold, enamel, semi-precious stones,
      diamonds, rubies, sapphires, pearls, silver,
      platinum
    H: all ca. ¾ to ⅞ inches
    Marks: KF, Fedor Afanassiev, Erik Kollin,
      August Holström, Alfred Thieleman,
      Mikhail Perkhin, Henrik Wigström,
      Gustav Lundell, assay marks mostly of
      St. Petersburg
    The Forbes Magazine Collection, New York

20. Snowflake Brooch-pendant
    Platinized silver, diamonds, gold
    Diam.: ¹⁵/₁₆ inches

Marks: Initials of workmaster A.
  Holmström, assay mark of St.
  Petersburg 1896-1908, inv. no. 73647
Private Collection, New York

21. Snowflake Brooch-pendant
    Platinized silver, diamonds, gold
    Diam.: ¹⁵/₁₆ inches
    Marks: Initials of workmaster A.
      Holmström, assay mark of St.
      Petersburg 1896-1908, inv. no. 73647
    Private Collection, New York

22. Lapel Watch
    Gold, enamel, diamonds
    H: 2⅛ inches
    Marks: Initials of workmaster August
      Holmström (?)
    Private Collection, NY

23. Imperial Presentation Cufflinks
    Gold, enamel, rubies, diamonds
    Marks: Initials of workmaster August
      Hollming, assay mark of St. Petersburg
      1896-1908
    Original fitted case
    Dorothy Kingery, Estate of James A.
      Williams

24. Imperial Presentation Cufflinks
    Gold, enamel, diamonds
    Marks: Initials of workmaster Alfred
      Thieleman
    Original fitted case
    Dorothy Kingery, Estate of James A.
      Williams

25. Pike-shaped Bowl
    Silver
    L: 23¾ inches
    Marks: Imperial Warrant, assay mark
      of Moscow 1896, assay master L.O.,
      inv. no. 6549
    Gerald M. de Sylvar

26. Dachshund Pitcher
    Silver
    L: 14½ inches
    Marks: Fabergé, initials of workmaster
      Julius Rappoport, assay mark of
      St. Petersburg before 1896
    Fitted case stamped "Russian Imperial
      Treasures Inc. The Schaffer Collection"
    Geri Forrester

27. Imperial Presentation Box
    Nephrite, gold, enamel, diamonds

W: 3⅜ inches
Marks: Fabergé, initials of workmaster
  Mikhail Perkhin, assay mark of
  St. Petersburg 1896-1908
Original fitted case
Private Collection, New York

28. Vase in Renaissance-style Mount
    Nephrite, gold, enamel, rubies, diamonds
    H: 10 inches
    Marks: Fabergé, initials of workmaster
      Mikhail Perkhin, assay mark of
      St. Petersburg 1896-1908
    Original price tag for 3250 rubles, inv. no.
      4400
    Original fitted case stamped with
      Imperial Warrant, St. Petersburg,
      Moscow
    Courtesy A La Vieille Russie, New York

29. Circular Tray
    Nephrite, gold, enamel, diamonds
    W: 10¾ (at handles)
    Marks: Fabergé, initials of workmaster
      Mikhail Perkhin, assay mark of St.
      Petersburg before 1896
    John Traina, San Francisco

30. Twenty-fifth Anniversary Clock
    Nephrite, gold, silver gilt, enamel,
      diamonds, pearls
    H: 6 inches
    Marks: Initials of workmaster Henrik
      Wigström, assay mark of St. Petersburg
      1908-17, inv. no. 18008
    The Forbes Magazine Collection, New York

31. Balletta Vase
    Topaz, gold
    H: 7⅞ inches
    Marks: Fabergé, initials of workmaster
      Mikhail Perkhin, assay mark of St.
      Petersburg 1896-1908
    Original fitted case stamped with
      Imperial Warrant
    The Brooklyn Museum, NY, bequest of
      Helen B. Sanders, 78.129.18 a-b

32. Imperial Basket of Lilies of the Valley
    Gold, silver, nephrite, pearls, diamonds
    H: 7½ inches, L: 8½ inches
    Marks: Fabergé, initials of workmaster
      August Hollming, assay mark
      of St. Petersburg before 1896; inscribed
      on base: "To Her Imperial Majesty,
      Czarina Alexandra Feodorovna, from
      the ironworks management and dealers

in the Siberian iron section of the
Pan-Russian Artistic and Manufac-
turing Exhibition in the year of 1896"
Original fitted case with the Czarina's
cipher on blue guilloché enamel field
New Orleans Museum of Art,
The Matilda Geddings Gray Foundation
Collection

33. Dandelion (Puff Ball)
Asbestos fiber, diamonds, gold,
nephrite, rock crystal
H: 7½ inches
The Brooklyn Museum, NY, bequest of
Helen B. Sanders, 78.129.17 a-b

34. Japanese Floral Composition
Nephrite, eosite, gold, enamel, diamonds,
copper
H: 6¼ inches
Marks: Inv. no. 5621
Original fitted case stamped with
Imperial Warrant, St. Petersburg,
Moscow
Courtesy A La Vieille Russie, New York

35. Five Floral Compositions, Cranberries,
Forget-me-nots, Two Lilies of the Valley,
and Wild Rose.
Russian semi-precious stones, gold, silver-
gilt, enamel, diamonds, pearls
H: from 2 to 4¾ inches
The Cleveland Museum of Art, The India
Early Minshall Collection 66.446, 66.444,
66.443, 66.445, 66.440

36. Cornflowers
Gold, silver, enamel, glass
H: 8¼ inches
New Orleans Museum of Art, The Matilda
Geddings Gray Foundation Collection

37. Frog on Agate Stand
Serpentine, agate, diamonds, silver
H: 4½ inches
Marks: Engraved initials KF under base
de Guigné Collection

38. Draft Horse
Marble, sapphires
H: 3⅛ inches
de Guigné Collection

39. Dancing Bear
Lapis lazuli, diamonds, silver
H: 4 inches
Private Collection, New York

40. Russian Peasant Girl
Purpurine, eosite, chalcedony, agate, jade,
sapphires
H: 6¼ inches
Marks: C. Fabergé engraved in English
under sole of one slipper
Original fitted case
The Metropolitan Museum of Art,
New York, Gift of R. Thornton Wilson
in memory of Florence Ellsworth
Wilson, 54.147.107

41. Sailor
Lapis lazuli, sapphires, onyx, aventurine,
jadeite
H: 4¾ inches
Original fitted case
Virginia Museum of Fine Arts, bequest of
Lillian Thomas Pratt, 47.20.268

42. Imperial Gray Enameled Presentation
Cigarette Case
Silver gilt, enamel, ruby, emerald,
sapphire, diamond
L: 3⅝ inches
Marks: Fabergé, initials of workmaster
August Hollming, assay mark of St.
Petersburg 1908–17
John Traina, San Francisco

43. Imperial Red Enameled Presentation
Cigarette Case
Silver gilt, enamel, diamonds, ruby,
sapphire
L: 3¾ inches
Marks: Fabergé, initials of workmaster
August Hollming, assay mark of St.
Petersburg 1908–17
Original fitted case
John Traina, San Francisco

44. Diamond-shaped Clock
Gold, silver gilt, enamel, seed pearls, ivory
W: 3½ inches
Marks: Fabergé, initials of workmaster
Mikhail Perkhin, assay mark of St.
Petersburg before 1896
Private Collection, California

45. Imperial Coronation Box
Gold, enamel, diamonds
L: 3¾ inches
Marks: Fabergé, initials of workmaster
August Holmström, assay mark of
St. Petersburg before 1896, inv. no. 1067
The Forbes Magazine Collection, New York

46. *Style-moderne* Clock
Gold, enamel, silver, seed pearls
H: 5 inches
Marks: Fabergé initials of workmaster
Henrik Wigström, assay mark of
St. Petersburg 1896–1908; plaque inscribed
"Murochka/on her birthday/18 May
1907/Mirra"
The Forbes Magazine Collection, New York

47. Aesthetic-movement Cigarette Case
Gold, enamel, diamonds, sapphire
L: 3½ inches
Marks: assay mark of Moscow before 1896,
inv. no. 11366
The Forbes Magazine Collection, New York

48. Miniature Louis XVI Chair
Gold, silver gilt, enamel, rubies, diamonds
H: 4⅛ inches
Marks: Fabergé, Imperial Warrant, assay
marks of Moscow 1896–1908, assay
master Ivan Lebedkin, inv. no. 25196
The Cleveland Museum of Art, The
India Early Minshall Collection, 66.454

49. Miniature Sedan Chair
Gold, enamel, rock crystal
H: 3½ inches
Marks: Fabergé, initials of workmaster
Mikhail Perkhin, assay mark of
St. Petersburg, 1896–1908, assay master
Iakov Liapunov
The Forbes Magazine Collection, New York

50. Fire-screen Frame
Gold, enamel, pearls
H: 7⅛ inches
Marks: Fabergé, initials of workmaster
Henrik Wigström, assay mark of
St. Petersburg 1908–17
The Forbes Magazine Collection, New York

51. Yusupov Music Box
Gold, pearls, enamel
L: 3½ inches
Marks: Fabergé, initials of workmaster
Henrik Wigström
Hillwood Museum, Washington, D.C., 11.80

52. Imperial Polar Star Clock
Gold, enamel, nephrite, silver, diamonds
H: 5¼ inches
Marks: Fabergé, initials of workmaster
Mikhail Perkhin, assay mark of St.
Petersburg before 1896, inv. no. 546591
The Forbes Magazine Collection, New York